The Joy of Stress

THE JOY OF STRESS

by *Pamela Pettler*

ILLUSTRATIONS
BY JACK ZIEGLER

 Quill
New York   1984

Library of Congress Cataloging in Publication Data

Pettler, Pamela.
The joy of stress.

1. Stress (Psychology)   2. Stress (Psychology)—
Anecdotes, facetiae, satire, etc.   I. Title.
BF575.S75P47   1984   155.9'2   83-17776
ISBN 0-688-02618-4 (pbk.)

Printed in the United States of America

First Edition

1 2 3 4 5 6 7 8 9 10

BOOK DESIGN BY PATTY LOWY

Contents

The Joy
of Stress

Introduction

How many times have you thought—if only I could be tense. If only I could be crippled by anxiety. If only I could be paralyzed by nameless and irrational fears.

Stress! Everywhere you look, it seems, other people are experiencing it. Articles, books, TV programs even talk about reducing it. Too *much* stress? Wait a minute! How come everyone seems to be ignoring the most basic question of all:

How do you get stress to begin with?

Now, for the first time, there is an answer. Here, in this book, the basic Principles of Stress— the fruits of years of dedicated, hands-on research —are laid out simply and clearly, from the most basic uses of Failure and Self-hate to the highly sophisticated concept of Praise as a Source of Stress.

Are you rich? neat? non-Jewish? Don't worry! Stress is democracy in its purest form. It knows no boundaries of class, creed, or closet space. You need no special equipment, no money (the less the better, God knows)—not even a willingness to learn. In fact, obstinate closed-mindedness is a *prime* source of stress for all parties concerned!

Yes, no matter how contented, how organized, how even-tempered you may be, you too can learn to be anxious and tense. You too can experience high blood pressure, low sex drive, and driving an extra fifty miles because you forgot to double-check the lock on the front door.

Just by using, or resisting, these basic techniques—you too can experience the Joys of Stress.

Part One

Stress

THE
BASIC
CONCEPTS

The "Karma" of Stress: Failure and Self-hate

JUST as the ancient samurai steeled themselves for battle by developing a fierce inner self-awareness, you too must arm yourself in your quest for stress by cultivating a profound, unshakable belief in your own hideous inadequacies.

We call this the "karma" of stress, and though it may seem difficult at first, you can soon learn to carry these thoughts with you wherever you go, and to apply them to almost any situation.

The Five Moans of Failure

(1) I am a failure.
(2) I am no good.
(3) Nothing I ever do will ever be any good.

13

(4) Everyone else knows this and is laughing
   at me.

(5) Everyone else does everything perfectly.

Repeat these thoughts to yourself, moaning softly.
Repeat them over and over. (Remember, obses-
sion is the friend of stress!) Learn to internalize
them, so that you are hardly even aware of their
presence.

Soon you will be able to apply them to any
situation:

Lunch with a Superior at Work
"I will order wrong."
"I will be dressed wrong."
"I will have spinach between my teeth."

An Important Date
"I won't be able to think of anything to say."
"I will be able to think of things to say, but
   they will be the wrong things."
"I will have spinach between my teeth."

Go over and over every failure (even the smallest).
Constantly remind yourself of how many things
you have done poorly in the past and in how many
ways you can fail in the future.

Remember, defeatism and self-hate are useful tools in any context, even success:

The Five Responses to Success

(1) It's a fluke.
(2) It can't last.
(3) It's a mistake.

And, furthermore,

(4) I am getting unfair recognition and my co-workers will hate me.
(5) Now I *really* can never live up to their expectations.

(The fact is, you probably don't need to worry much about success, especially once you've mastered the next two chapters.) In an emergency, you can always add a little pep talk: "Okay, so you won the Pulitzer Prize. Now what?"

Finally, apply these basic attitudes to your *outward* manifestation—your sadly repellent physical appearance. Here we use an elementary self-examination.

Basic self-hatred

Look at your nose in the mirror. It's getting bigger, isn't it? The nose is the only part of your body that keeps growing, you know. Check it out again. How about in profile? I'm surprised it even *fits* on the mirror.

How about your hands? Not so youthful-looking anymore, are they? What about that "freckle"? Who're you kidding, liver-spot-face?

Back to the mirror. What about those little wrinkles around your eyes? Getting deeper, aren't they? How about that new one?

Hey! Is that another *gray hair?*

Soon you should be able to tailor this to your own personal appearance.

Remember, failure and self-hatred are the cornerstones of stress! (For more information, you may wish to consult my trilogy, *Failing at Work, Failing at Home,* and *Failing en Route from Work to Home.*)

**STRESS GRAND MASTER—
MOTION-PICTURE DIVISION**
"I don't like my writing. I like almost nothing I have ever written. As a rule, I don't ever go back and look at what I've written because it is too embarrassing."

—WILLIAM GOLDMAN, two-time Academy Award-winner and author of *Marathon Man* and *Butch Cassidy and The Sundance Kid*, in *The Craft of the Screenwriter*

Being Perfect

A CLOSE relative of Failure and Self-hate, Relentless Perfectionism is one of the most popular stress concepts. It is spare, almost elegant in its simplicity: *You must be perfect.*

If you want to be loved, happy, and successful, you have to be the best, the fastest, and the smartest. *All the time.*

You should be working, or thinking about working, at every possible moment. Thoughts like "I don't have enough years left," "I can never make up that time I wasted in my twenties," and "I wish there were three of me" should dominate your waking moments.

And, of course, your goals must be higher and far more extensive than anyone else's. Only ordinary people have ordinary goals.

Sample Goals

(1) Winning the Nobel Prize
(2) Winning the Iron Man
(3) Achieving personal worth of twenty million dollars
(4) All of the above
(5) All of the above before the age of twenty-one

If you don't reach your goals—all of them—better, sooner, and more spectacularly than anyone else—*you have failed.*

It doesn't matter if you're good, or very good, or even very, very good. It doesn't matter how much other people may admire you. *You* know the yawning abyss between what you're doing and the way it *should* be.

**STRESS GRAND MASTER—
ART DIVISION**
"I am always filled with remorse, terribly so, when I think of my work as so little in keeping with what I should have liked to do."

—VINCENT VAN GOGH, in his autobiography

STRESS GRAND MASTER—
DANCE DIVISION
"I am full of faults."

—FRED ASTAIRE, in *his*
autobiography

They're Getting Ahead of You

A True Story

One day in late 1969, in the research library of the University of California at Berkeley, a young man went berserk. He ran through the library, shouting hysterically at his astonished fellow students, "Stop! Stop! You're getting ahead of me!"

He was arrested. But what was his crime, really? *Being in the wrong decade.* As we all know, the sixties era, and its childish preoccupation with peace, good sex, and battered VW buses, was little more than a black mark, a shameful demerit in the History of Stress.

Now, of course, in the stress-filled eighties, this concept of "getting ahead of me" has regained its rightful place of importance. In fact, it is one of the basic precepts of stress.

Simply stated, *people are getting ahead of you*. All the time.

While you're at your desk, people working out at the gym are getting ahead of you.

While you're at the gym, your co-workers are getting ahead of you.

If a friend gets a promotion at work, she has gotten ahead of you.

If a colleague reads a book you haven't read, he has gotten ahead of you.

The entire U.S. swim team has gotten ahead of you.

While you're reading this book, *everyone* is getting ahead of you.

The beauty of this concept is that it can be applied across the board, anywhere, anytime.

On the road? Drivers of more expensive cars have gotten ahead of you.

Watching TV? All the writers, actors, and technical crews have gotten ahead of you.

At Marine World? The *dolphins* have gotten ahead of you.

Always judge yourself, and your intrinsic moral worth, in terms of specific achievements as compared to others.

Always judge any situation in relation to how

much the people involved have gotten ahead of you, and in what ways.

**STRESS GRAND MASTER—
SPORTS DIVISION**
"When you are not
practicing, remember,
someone somewhere is
practicing, and when you
meet him, he will win."

—"EASY ED" MACAULEY,
youngest player ever* to be
elected to the pro Basketball
Hall of Fame

---

*He got ahead of you, didn't he?

WELL, there you have it. Unforgiving perfectionism, an ever-expanding awareness of your irredeemable flaws as a human being, and habitual, ghastly comparison between yourself and others. The *Basic Stress Attitude*. Be sure to master this attitude before continuing.

"What if I feel that I will never be able to master these, or any other, basics?" you may ask.

Good! A constant, gnawing feeling of inadequate mastery of fundamental concepts is an *excellent* way to begin!

Keeping that in mind, let us now move on to "Stress: The Specifics."

Part Two

STRESS THE SPECIFICS

Exercise Your Way to Stress

Y ou can't always be at the dentist's or studying for the bar exam. That's why we've developed these quick Stress Exercises—a short, comprehensive workout that can be done anywhere, anytime—at your desk (for a quick sapping of any unexpected energy), at home (where much relaxation often occurs).

THE BASIC STRESS WORKOUT

Stand, or slouch in a soft, awkward chair. Open your eyes, breathe rapidly, and concentrate.

- Wiggle your feet. They ache, don't they? Have you ever thought it might be a deformity in your foot? What about that numbness you sometimes get? You can't really feel your little toe right now, can you?

- Travel mentally up to your knees. What about that nagging pain? Maybe you walked too much today and dried out the cartilage. What exactly is "water on the knee"?
- Notice the actual length of your legs. Women may want to consider Cyd Charisse. Men might think of the average NBA salary.
- Now, of course, your genitalia. Need we say more?
- Moving above the waist—that little bump on your back. Are you sure it's just a zit? It's gotten bigger, hasn't it?
- Now, your abdominal area. Try to feel each and every one of your internal organs. Your gallbladder. (What about that strange pain you've been getting?) Your liver. (Or is it there?) The membranes of your stomach lining— Wait! Is that a twinge of appendicitis? What about that shortness of breath? Has one of your lungs collapsed? Your heart—should it be going that fast? It's racing, isn't it? It just skipped a beat, didn't it? What about that pain down your left arm? Those burning sensations? That tightness across your chest—

—see? You're tense already, aren't you? With a little practice you can slip into this exercise without even thinking.

In addition to the basic workout, you might

30

want to add a few "spot" inducers. That's why we've also included these "Stressometrics."

STRESSOMETRICS

Head and neck. Lean head slightly forward. Tense neck. Hold.

Eyes and mouth. Frown. Squint. Tense jaw. Hold.

Hands and fingers. Clench fist. Hold.

Legs, thighs, and abdomen. Jiggle leg. Repeat.

Neck and back. Twist around, bending toward floor, and try to pull piece of paper out from under the chair you are sitting on.

If you have a little more time, you may want to incorporate the more time-consuming long-range exercise into your schedule. Remember, your *attitude* is what's important.

LONG-RANGE EXERCISE

Walking. Why is that man following you? What about that guy loitering on the corner? And the guy driving his car so slowly? What if a truck jumps the curb and kills you?

Running. All of the above, and shin splints.

Swimming. Drowning.

Weight machines. Will tear tiny but crucial muscle in back and will never be able to walk again.

Aerobic dance. Everyone is laughing at you.

31

Sex

AFTER a pleasant dinner by candlelight, Gordon and Gladys sit on the couch in front of a roaring fire. At almost the same moment, they turn to each other with that special smile. Both are feeling the first stirrings of desire. Gordon reaches up to unbutton Gladys's blouse, exposing her luscious creamy bosom. "You're so beautiful," he murmurs. Gladys glides her hand downward, her dainty fingers eagerly reaching for her partner's large, engorged—

—well, *need* I go on! You *get* the idea. Gordon and Gladys (not their real names) are *nonstressed sex partners*. Like many others, they have trapped themselves in a vicious circle of relaxed, frequent sex.

Perhaps you share their situation. If so, don't worry. With just a little help you can learn to have sex the way millions of other Americans do. Just remember these five basic points:

(1) Sex *is* a performance. You are being judged at all times, and given a grade (A, B, C, D, and No Credit). (There is no Pass/Fail option.)
(2) Penis size *is* all-important: 10, 12 inches at least, or forget it. It's not what you do with it, it's how big it is.
(3) Female sex organs *are* peculiar-looking and should be kept hidden at all times.
(4) Orgasm is required for any woman wishing to receive a passing grade.
(5) Your partner *can* smell your breath.

Mood Music for Stressed Sex

Threnody for the Victims of Hiroshima (Penderecki)
A Survivor from Warsaw (Schönberg)
Isle of the Dead (Rachmaninoff)
Funeral March (Chopin)
Requiem (Mozart)
Requiem (Verdi)
Requiem (Brahms)
Taps
Car alarm
Air-raid siren

Flying:
A Crash Course

ARE you a pink-knuckled flier? Do you break out into a warm smile at the sight of an airplane? Do you read peacefully or even *look out the window* as the plane takes off, banking steeply through mercurial updrafts?

Don't despair! There are thousands of people like you, and with just a little help and the power of your own mental processes, you too can learn to appreciate flying as the hideous, terrifying experience it really is.

THE PHYSICS OF FLYING

Let's begin at the beginning. Before you even get on that plane, try to grasp the basic principles involved.

What does the plane fly on? *Air*. What is air? Air is *nothing*. We breathe this stuff into our *lungs*. There is no possible way for air to support a twelve-ton hunk of aluminum. Does air support your briefcase? Your garment bag? Of course not! Otherwise you could just send them on ahead and forget the whole thing!

Before takeoff

On the plane, closely inspect the tube that is likely to be your aluminum coffin. Look at the other passengers. Are these the people you want to die with?

The NO SMOKING sign is on, reminding you that you are enclosed with thousands of gallons of highly flammable fuel. Keep in mind how many sparks are generated as an airplane accelerates to takeoff!

Taxiing

As the plane begins to taxi, the pilot comes on the intercom. Listen closely. Do you detect a drunken slur?

Are the stewardesses relaxed and smiling? Remember, they are paid to smile *no matter what*.

Takeoff

As you hurtle down the runway toward probable incineration, you may still feel slightly relaxed. But remember, crash reports usually read, "Moments after takeoff . . ." "Moments after liftoff . . ." or "Moments after the great doomed bird shuddered skyward . . ."

It may help to keep this explanatory chart in mind:

Noises During Takeoff	*Explanation*
Bumps on runway	Wheel falling off
Jolts as plane takes off	Engine falling off
Loud whirring noise	Landing gear falling off
Bump or shudder	Cargo door falling off
Change in sound after takeoff	Engine failure
Change in speed after takeoff	Engine failure
Movement of wing flaps	Pilot's last desperate attempt to accommodate engine failure; also, signal to other aircraft to keep away
Change in direction	Plane banking suddenly in futile attempt to avoid collision

Ascending too rapidly	Plane cannot get nose down and will inevitably stall, diving to ground
Ascending too slowly	Plane cannot get up enough speed (probably due to engine failure) and will inevitably stall, plummeting to ground

IN FLIGHT

During the flight, it's hard for even the most veteran worriers to remain tense, especially since alcohol has twice its usual potency at high altitudes (not that the plane is going to be able to *maintain* any sort of altitude).

There's always the possibility of lightning, air pockets, fires started in the cooking areas, and mid-air collisions. But you might also want to think about:

(1) *The High and the Mighty*
(2) The *Twilight Zone* episode where William Shatner saw the gremlin *right outside his window*
(3) *William Shatner* right outside your window
(4) The bottom falling out of the airplane

plunging you thousands of feet downward through the murky darkness (In anticipation of this, always keep your shoes on.)

LANDING

This is the flip side (to use an appropriate term) to takeoff, and the other major source of stories beginning "Witnesses said . . ." Again, an understanding of physics will help you to appreciate the basic possibilities:

(1) Plane is too high and will miss the runway.
(2) Plane is too low and will plow into the runway.
(3) Plane is too fast and will skid off the runway into the (aptly named) terminal buildings.
(4) Rain, see (3).
(5) Gust of wind will slam plane into ground.
(6) Gust of wind will throw plane into tailspin, then slam it into ground.

In the event of water approaches, well, let's just hope you can swim. (See "Exercise Your Way to Stress.")

ON THE GROUND

Once you are inside the terminal building (with luck, *after* having deplaned), there is still the likelihood of *another* plane encountering numbers (3) or (4) above, and crashing into you in the building.

Outside the building, of course, the surrounding airspace is littered with aircraft struggling to take off or land. Don't forget that as a plane crashes, it leaves a fiery wasteland in its wake, crushing people on the ground in a smoky, molten mass of debris!

Finally, remember, no matter where you are, a piece of fuselage can always fall off a plane, crashing unexpectedly through the roof of the very building you just happen to be in—anywhere, anytime! *You never know!*

**STRESS GRAND MASTER
AHEAD OF HIS TIME**
"Me miserable! which way
   shall I fly
Infinite wrath, and infinite
   despair?
Which way I fly is hell . . ."

—JOHN MILTON, *Paradise Lost*

The Two Basic
Stress-Food Groups

THE two basic stress-food groups are *coffee* and *chocolate*. Oh, sure, there are a few diehard eccentrics who swear by chili peppers or triple-cream pastries, especially when eaten at the same time.

But experts have repeatedly proved that the purest and most immediate stress foods are the old standbys, coffee and chocolate. They are outstanding for their amazing dual function: Not only do you turn to them naturally (and with increasing urgency) in times of stress, but the caffeine and sugar actually *enhance* and *expand* your stressful feelings even as you ingest them!

COFFEE

Coffee, of course, is the prime stress food. Ideally, you should chain-drink it, but at *least* sixteen or seventeen cups must be consumed daily. You should be *drinking* or *thinking* about coffee at any given point of the day or night.

These few basic tips should help you on your way:

(1) Taste-test, and find unsatisfactory, every coffee bean available in your city, your state, and throughout the Americas. Consider starting a small coffee plantation of your own.

(2) Buy only the best support equipment. A Braun grinder. A Krups coffeemaker. Never mind what they did during the war.

(3) Buy larger and larger mugs.

(4) Get so that the sight of Tom Selleck pouring himself a cup of coffee creates intense physical desire—for the coffee.

(5) Judge friends, work situations, and the politics of multinational corporations entirely by the quality of the coffee served.

CHOCOLATE

or "Need I say more?"
Hershey bars. Hot-fudge sundaes. Fudge brownies.
Fudge. Chocolate mousse. Chocolate soufflé.
Devil's food cake. Chocolate truffles. Teuscher's
chocolate truffles. Switzerland.

A Chocolate Poem

Who needs Kirk or Marlon or Clindt
When you've got Suchard, Tobler, and Lindt?

Three Ways to Think of Chocolate

(1) As a reward for having done something
good
(2) As a consolation for having done something bad
(3) As a diversion from not having done anything at all

The Stress
Diet

THE stress diet begins with a form of behavior modification, Aversion Therapy—here, aversion to *yourself*.

Get out that old bathing suit and take a long look at yourself, preferably in front of one of those three-way mirrors. Examine yourself from all angles, twisting around as much as your rolls of fat will allow.

Whisper viciously to yourself: "Look at those thighs. Have you ever seen anything so disgusting?" Laugh derisively: "What's that? 'Pleasantly plump'? Dream *on*, hogface!"

Good! Now that you've established the correct attitude, you are ready to begin your new diet.

THE STRESSER'S DIET

Breakfast
½ grapefruit
1 piece whole-wheat toast
8 oz. skim milk

Lunch
4 oz. lean broiled chicken
1 cup steamed lima beans
1 Oreo cookie
Herb tea

Midafternoon snack
Rest of the package of Oreo cookies
Quart of rocky-road ice cream
Jar of hot-fudge sauce

Dinner
2 loaves garlic bread
Large mushroom-and-pepperoni pizza
Large pitcher of beer
3 Milky Ways
Entire frozen cheesecake, eaten directly out
    of the freezer

The best part about this diet is that you never feel
hungry at the end of the day!

As you can see, this diet consists of two lev-
els—punitive deprivation and sodden remorse.
Notice that you are actually eating everything you
want, but not enjoying a single mouthful!

A few little "dieter's tricks" will help you on your way—

(1) Pick a good weight goal—what you weighed when you were eleven, perhaps.
(2) Weigh yourself two or three times a day.
(3) Pin up little hints to yourself, like that picture of yourself in your sweat suit, also known as the "hippo" picture.
(4) Wear clothes in the size you *should* be. That "whalebone corset" feeling will be a constant reminder—if you weren't such a pig, those clothes would fit you.
(5) As you eat, use strong mental imagery— vultures diving on their prey, or ravenous wolves gulping their food for the winter.

It also helps to keep the fridge stocked with handy snacks:

(1) Chocolate-chip cookie dough
(2) Homemade potato salad
(3) Leftover lasagna
(4) Package of fresh jelly doughnuts
(5) Swiss-chocolate-almond ice cream
(6) Chocolate Easter bunnies or chocolate Santas (in season)

And yes, you *can* eat out on this diet! Some good restaurant choices might be:

(1) Pancake houses
(2) Smorgasbords

(3) "All you can eat" champagne brunches
(4) Any restaurant with unlimited bread on the table

And finally, although it isn't necessary, it's always helpful to have a supportive spouse. A true stress spouse will diet *with* you, and will encourage you with phrases such as "Come on, butterball," "Here, Bossie," or simply "Sooooo-eeeee!"

Parties—The Horror, the Horror . . .

PARTIES, of course, are bountiful sources of stress. No matter which side you are on (and it's always useful to think of parties as having "sides," as at the Battle of Agincourt), there are innumerable paths to stress's allies: anxiety and panic. Whether you are the hopelessly inept host or the dreadful inert-gaslike guest, you can easily experience (or create) a whole series of desperately dismal evenings!

Let's begin with the less likely possibility—you're a guest. Someone slipped up, or wants something from you, and you were invited. You'll probably begin with the Five Guest Panics:

(1) You'll go on the wrong day.
(2) You'll go to the wrong house.

(3) You'll be too early.

(4) You'll be too late.

(5) You'll be right on time but the terrible neurotic host will be unprepared and you'll have to engage in frozen conversation for hours before anyone else shows up.

These, of course, are mere preliminary bagatelles. Beyond them lies something far more significant, your single most important act as a guest: *your entrance to the party*. As always, the key is *correct mental attitude*. Think of your entrance as your gateway to the evening, if not to the rest of your life. Focus on a strong internal image of yourself— perhaps a water buffalo or a large gorilla—as you shamble in, grunting and snorting. Remember, everyone is watching you, and your entire future happiness depends on this moment!

At the party, look around you. You're incorrectly dressed, aren't you? And, of course, you don't know anyone. The others have all known each other since grade school. Even now, as they chat in cliquish codes and use pet animal names for each other, they are watching you and laughing as you fumble at inept small talk. Perhaps you have even been invited for their personal amusement!

Later, as you skulk over to the hors d'oeuvres in a flimsy attempt to appear purposeful, everyone will be saying, "Oh, Bunny, do look at the fat girl over by the clam dip. Did you *ever*?"

> **SMALL-TALK GAMBITS FOR THE STRESSER**
> (1) "Ehhhhhhhhh . . . . . ."
> (2) "Arrrrrr . . . ."
> (3) High-pitched, over-eager laughter
> (4) Choking on a piece of cauliflower

If you're the host, of course, you have only the One Host Panic:

(1) No one will come.

This is sometimes augmented by the sub-panics:

(1a) Your guests will be too early.
(1b) Your guests will be too late.
(1c) Your first guest will be this terrible neurotic who shows up right on time and you'll have to engage in frozen conversation for hours before anyone else shows up.

In addition, during the party, there are any number of splendid opportunities for creating a whole pageant of entertainment disasters:

(1) As always, you will be incorrectly dressed.
(2) You will run out of food and drink.
(3) You will poison your guests with your

hors d'oeuvres, and maybe even some of the oeuvres, too.

(4) You will set fire to the kitchen and set off the smoke alarm.

(5) Your guest of honor won't show up.

(6) Your guest of honor will show up, drunk.

(7) Your guest of honor will get into a fist-fight.

(8) Your guest of honor will get into a gun-fight.

(9) Your guest of honor's gunfight will disturb your Mafia neighbors (see chapter on "Noise").

Most likely, though, none of the above will happen. What will really occur is that after about thirty minutes, your few sparse guests will settle into a deadly, staring silence. With luck, word will get out, and your parties will soon be known affectionately as "vacuums," "existential nightmares," or simply "black holes."

Despite all your efforts, of course, there's always the chance that, as either guest or host, you may momentarily delude yourself into imagining some fleeting party success. In such a case keep in mind the true stresser's response to such a situation:

**STRESS GRAND MASTER—
NORTHERN-LIGHTS DIVISION**
"I have just returned from a
party of which I was the life
and soul; witty banter
flowed from my lips,
everyone laughed and
admired me. I came away
wanting to shoot myself."

—Sören "The Party Animal"
    Kierkegaard, diary entry

The Somnia Syndrome

Do you relax immediately after going to bed? Do you find yourself drifting off, despite careful avoidance of warm milk, hot baths, or mild exercise before retiring? Are you asleep within fifteen minutes? If so, you may be one of the millions of Americans who suffer from *somnia*.

Somnia, the inability to lie awake long into the night, is surprisingly widespread. But you will be glad to hear that it's *not* incurable. In fact, it can be very easily overcome, with just a few simple techniques.

Remember, sleep is *learned* and can just as easily be *unlearned*.

BEFORE GOING TO BED

- Use the bedroom for *non-sleep-related* activities. Pay bills. Examine yourself for early warning signs of cancer. Make awkward phone calls to former co-workers to ask them for references. Argue. If you live alone, argue with yourself. (If possible, do all of these while actually *in* bed.)
- Eat several heavy, spicy meals.
- Watch *Psycho, The Texas Chain-Saw Massacre,* or, if you live in a rural area, *In Cold Blood.*

WARNING: Under *no* circumstance should you watch your PBS channel!

AFTER GOING TO BED

Your basic task here is to learn to control your thoughts. Yes, you *can* learn to monitor your own mental processes! Choose your topics carefully. This is an excellent time to worry about financial problems, job difficulties, and exactly when and how you will die. Think about how your skin rots away after you're dead, leaving a grinning skeleton which itself soon crumbles to dust. Probe your face to feel your skeleton.

Or you might want to concentrate on specific issues:

(1) What's that funny noise?

(2) Where in the apartment should you hide when the Nazis come to get you?

(3) What is the best route out of the city in the event of nuclear holocaust?

(4) What would you do if your spouse died?

(5) Is your spouse in fact still breathing? (Poke spouse to make sure.)

If none of these suggestions works, and you find yourself drifting off, just think about what they told you when Nana died. "She just went to sleep and *never woke up*." Remember? Still feel sleepy?

Perhaps you'd prefer to conjure up an entire scenario:

Sample Scenario

You're driving your car, stopped at a stoplight. Suddenly, a truck smashes into your rear, plowing you into the car in front! Your car bursts into flames! Groggy from the impact, you struggle to escape, but the door is mangled and you can't get out! With your broken arm, you painfully roll down the window—but your seat belt is stuck! Fused by the flames! You can't move! The flames roar towards you!

Remember, if you find yourself dwelling on images of deep green forests, quiet snow-covered mountains, or crystal-clear mountain lakes, *sit up.* Tell yourself, "Stop!" Concentrate on your surroundings. Surely there is some strange noise or smell you can focus on. In time you may even learn to have heartwarming experiences like the one illustrated here.

A True Story

One night around 2 A.M., Gloria (not her real name) became convinced that she smelled smoke. She checked through the whole apartment, even out the windows. Definitely a strong smell of smoke. And now that she thought about it, the smell was coming out of the heating vents!

Hesitantly, since he was a stranger to her, she phoned her downstairs neighbor, waking him up. But he agreed instantly. Not only did he smell smoke, but it seemed awfully warm in his apartment!

Gloria called the fire department, alerted the entire apartment house, got fully dressed, and went out to the street. Moments later, a huge red fire truck roared into the neighborhood, lights illuminating half the block. As the neighbors gawked, five asbestos-suited young firemen leaped off the truck with their equipment and hurried up to Gloria's apartment.

The smoke smell had vanished.

They checked the entire apartment, the hallways, and the furnace in the basement. There was no smoke smell anywhere.

Also, Gloria noticed that her downstairs neighbor was sort of peculiar. He grinned a lot and agreed with everything anyone said.

Inspirational, isn't it? Notice that this little story

contains all the elements necessary for the true stresser's fight against somnia. Not just anxiety, apprehension, and the all-important *getting out of bed and getting dressed*, but also the ever-desirable public embarrassment and humiliation!

How does this tale end, you may ask? Well, Gloria lamely tried to explain herself, feebly apologized to everyone, and slunk upstairs to her apartment, where she eventually returned to bed and shortly afterward began smelling smoke again.

**STRESS GRAND MASTER—
LITERATURE DIVISION**
[Thoughts written while trying to get to sleep]
"I see waste and horror—what I might have been and done that is lost, spent, gone, dissipated, unrecapturable . . . The horror has come now like a storm—what if this night prefigured the night after death—what if all thereafter was an eternal quivering on the edge of an abyss with everything bare and vicious in oneself urging one forward and the baseness and viciousness of the world just ahead. No choice, no road, no hope—only the endless repetition of the sordid and the semi-tragic."

—F. SCOTT FITZGERALD, in
"The Crack-Up"

Health Worries and
How to Get Them

VERY few stress inducers can claim the matchless symmetry of Gault's Theorem:

Health worries cause stress.
Stress causes health worries.

In your quest for stress, therefore, you have probably already found yourself *naturally* worrying about your health!

But in addition to vague, slapdash worries, it is also important to have a little knowledge. Remember, a little knowledge is a dangerous thing, and danger is the friend of stress!

This handy chart will provide you with a limited but potent knowledge of the early symptoms and warning signs of most major diseases. You may want to read up on some of the fatal ones. (The

Encyclopaedia Britannica can be counted on to provide extensive and gruesome details.)

The Symptoms	The Disease
Headache, throbbing	Brain tumor
Headache, stabbing	Brain tumor
Stiff neck	Brain tumor pressing on neck tumor
Toothache	Hidden abscess about to infect bloodstream
Backache	Final warning sign before complete paralysis
Dizziness	Brain swollen, about to disintegrate
Abdominal pain	Tumor the size of a grapefruit *
Shortness of breath	Collapsed lung
Fatigue	Leukemia
Itchy skin	Leprosy
Itchy eyes	Small seed caught in eye that will either work its way back into the brain or sprout into a small tree

* Notice that tumors are always "the size of a grapefruit," never "the size of a small wall safe" or "a portable electric coffee-maker."

Dull humming in ears	Going deaf
Bumps, rashes, or bruises anywhere on your body	Riddled with cancer
Cold hands	Poor circulation due to imminent heart failure
Heart skipping a beat	Heart failure

Now all you need to do is make sure you are unceasingly aware of even the tiniest changes in your bodily makeup. Constantly monitor the entire surface of your body.

Scratching your arm during a meeting, you may unexpectedly come upon that strange new rash. Shifting positions during lovemaking, you may suddenly feel that horrifying twinge right through your left leg. Frowning in disbelief as you watch a new sitcom, you may discover that unusual new throbbing in your forehead.

Remember, no matter where you are, conduct incessant self-examinations! You can discover that tiny fatal symptom at any time! Colleagues, lovers, and even passing acquaintances will soon become accustomed to the sight of you lurching suddenly upright, eyes glazed in panic.

> **STRESS GRAND MASTER—
> ODES DIVISION**
> "Think to yourself that every
> day is your last."
>
> —HORACE, *Epistles,* Book I

Don't forget, many people live to be one hundred, and if the national average is seventy, that means some of us have to kick off at forty! Come to think of it, you've been feeling kind of tired lately, haven't you?

FOR WOMEN ONLY: BREAST SELF-EXAMINATION

(1) Lie on your back, left hand behind head.
(2) With your right hand, examine your left breast. It's awfully lumpy in there, isn't it? Are you sure that's just regular breast tissue? What about here—and here— and— Wait! What's that! It's moving around! It is! It's a lump! Yes! A lump!
(3) With your left hand, wipe sweat off forehead.

Even if you've just been to the doctor and have been reassured that everything is completely normal—the true stresser's response here is "Sure, normal *today*. But what about *tomorrow*?"

There are only three things you can reasonably do:

(1) Memorize your breasts. (Give yourself surprise quizzes.)
(2) Buy a thermograph machine and carry it around with you for constantly ongoing mammographs.
(3) Hire a personal gynecologist who will examine you, and only you, twice a day.

Stomach Trouble— The Big Payoff

THE TRUE stresser has constant stomach trouble.

Yes, some stressers do claim headaches, and even point to impressive precedents such as Joan Didion or Zeus. But although headaches certainly have one crucial stress element—pain—they lack an even more important quality—*humiliation*. Let's face it—you can easily discuss a headache with colleagues, dates, or strangers. But even the briefest mention of stomach trouble immediately conjures up a hideously mortifying visual image. You'll notice Joan Didion doesn't write about her loose stools, does she?

And stomach trouble isn't just embarrassing; it's inconvenient! Look how a good case of the runs can add a whole new stress dimension to these common experiences:

Business meetings: Now you can be forced to excuse yourself and disappear for forty-five minutes, trapped groaning in the bathroom. Not only will you miss the meeting, allowing your rival to take credit for your best idea, but you will never be able to come up with a feasible excuse for being gone so long!

Social engagements: Now you can writhe in secret agony for hours rather than asking someone to turn up the radio!

Travel: Now you can spend the bulk (to use an appropriate term) of your trip hunting for functional public bathrooms! And if you stay at quaint country inns with the bathrooms down the hall, nothing beats tottering down a strange dark corridor at 2 A.M., one hand clutching your stomach, the other clutching a flashlight and the international edition of *Time* (long since memorized), praying the bathroom is unoccupied and that no one else will need it for the next thirty minutes!

And stomach cramps can strike at any moment! "A walk in the moonlight, Guido? How lovel—AUGHHHHHHHHHHH—why no, nothing's wrong!"

Soon you can discover uncharted regions of embarrassment and inconvenience. The possibilities are endless!

A *True Story*

Paris to London. It had not been a pretty flight. First, the airplane was so ancient that half the inside paneling fell off as soon as the passengers sat down. Then, in a needless fit of honesty, the pilot came on to announce "trouble firing up the third engine, ha-ha."

Gerda (not her real name) was not happy. Not only would takeoff be dicey, but the entire flight would be a grim bet against the third engine. Sure enough, takeoff was wretched, and the plane rolled and pitched all the way across the treacherous Channel air currents, finally bouncing to a haphazard stop at the end of a damp Heathrow runway.

As the other passengers disembarked, Gerda went for the aft lavatory.

But several minutes later the stewardess knocked and uttered those words of terror to any stomach-cramp-o-phile: "Excuse me, miss, you have to leave."

Gerda staggered out, hurried to the door of the plane, and then she saw, below her on the tarmac, a truly dreadful sight: the entire planeload of passengers, staring up at her, crammed into a bus ready to take them to the terminal. They had been standing there, quietly, horribly, like some ghastly Greek chorus, waiting for her while she sat in the plane above them.

Procrastination
as a Source of Stress

WE'LL get to this later.

How to Respond
to Praise

NYONE *who gives*
you praise is wrong.

There are only four reasons why anyone could
possibly praise you:

(1) They have no judgment whatsoever.
(2) They are just too kind to tell you the
truth.
(3) They are deliberately trying to lull you
into false self-confidence so they can
really get you later.
(4) They are just kidding and can't believe
that you would really believe them, and
now they are secretly laughing hysterically and can't wait to tell all their
friends.

Example

You complete a project at work. It is widely circulated throughout the company. Over the next few weeks you get these responses:

> Your mother: "It's terrific!" (Obviously, number 2, above)
> Colleagues: "It's terrific!" (Number 4)
> Your boss: "It's terrific!" (Number 3)
> Your spouse: (Who cares *what* she says? She obviously has no judgment anyway if she married *you*. Number 1 ex officio)

**STRESS GRAND MASTER—
SATIRIST DIVISION**
"Complimenting is lying."

—JONATHAN SWIFT, in
Polite Conversation

How to Take Rejection

**A**LWAYS *take rejection personally.*

Rejection *always* reflects deep-seated distaste, loathing, and often secret vendettas toward you, as well as the fact that, basically, nobody likes you.

Some Typical Rejections and Their Meanings:

"I won't be able to make our lunch date today."	"I hate you."
"I'm busy this Saturday night."	"I hate you."
"I didn't hear what you said."	"I hate you."
"I don't agree with you."	"I hate you."

"All our lines are busy at this time."   "We all hate you."

Soon you will be able to recognize that un-answered letters, unappreciated jokes, and even busy signals are all tokens of the same coin—hatred—and you'll be able to enjoy renewed stress and suffering in almost any personal encounter.

Useful Responses to Rejection

(1) Staying in bed for the rest of your life
(2) Eating

**STRESS GRAND MASTER—
CRIME-AND-PUNISHMENT
DIVISION
"Rejection is essential."**

—FËDOR DOSTOEVSKI,
Notebook IX

Negotiation

NEGOTIATION is, of course, a *Doppelstresser* (loosely translated, "double-stress-causer"). Here you can experience *both* stress by anticipation and stress by humiliation.

For example, let's say you're waiting to hear about a job offer. It's a nice little job—you wouldn't kick it out of bed—but it's not perfect, either. You resolve to negotiate for certain minimum conditions.

Fine! Establish firmly in your mind the minimum situation you would accept. Worry in depth about any possible demands they might make. Plan innumerable counterdemands, feints, and subtle strategies. Write everything down. Memorize everything. Practice repeatedly in front of the mirror. You're not going to be taken advantage of *this* time!

When they call, instantly capitulate. "A job at half the salary you originally offered and with no employee benefits? Gosh, thanks!" (Remember, you won't even have the justification of being caught off guard, so your humiliation and self-hate will be pure.)

Soon you can use these tactics in negotiating for anything—a higher salary, a better office, or even a bigger mirror.

Remember: No matter how well you prepare, no matter how much you practice, the other side will effortlessly, contemptuously sidestep you. Learn to think of yourself as a human Maginot Line, and the opposition as the German Panzers.

Inassertiveness Training

MEMORIZE these phrases:

"Anywhere you like"
"Anything you say"
"Whatever *you'd* like to do"

Proper application of these key phrases can induce the double stress of watching things go needlessly wrong *and* realizing you brought it on yourself by your own inassertiveness.

For more advanced practitioners, forelock tugging, obsequious bowing, and having WELCOME printed on your forehead are also popular options.

Visualizing Situations in Advance

VISUALIZING stress situations in advance is one of the oldest stress activities, and no wonder! Not only does it provide the much-desired Stress by Anticipation, but it also *intensifies* the stress of the situation when it actually does occur.

Why say "We'll cross that bridge when we come to it" when you can experience the crossing so many, many more times?

The trick is to imagine a situation exactly as it is most likely to occur, rationally and with no exaggeration. Here are two typical encounters.

VISUALIZING A JOB INTERVIEW

YOU: Hello, I'm Gordon Grimsdyke—

INTERVIEWER: *You!* I don't *believe* it! You *really came?*

YOU: Well, you did send me a letter—

INTERVIEWER: I really don't believe this! We just sent that letter as a *gag*! I mean, *no one* here could *believe* that ridiculous résumé—we thought the whole thing was a practical joke!

YOU: Well, actually, no, it wasn't—

INTERVIEWER: I can't believe you actually have the *presumption* to think we would even spend one *minute* thinking about you! My God! Get out of this office! You'll never work in this town again!

VISUALIZING ASKING FOR A RAISE

(Your boss, C.C., a ruddy man in a green golf sweater, is practicing his golf swings in his large, spacious office. You enter.)

C.C.: Yeah?

YOU: I, ah, well, I've been doing a lot of good work lately . . .

C.C.: You? Ha! Ha ha! Ha ha ha! (into intercom) Hey, J.T., get in here!

(J.T., a ruddy man in a red golf sweater, enters eagerly.)

YOU: . . . and I've been taking on more responsibilities . . .

J.T. (uproariously): Wait a dern minute! Is this about salary? Oh, Lord, C.C., you didn't *warn* me!

(C.C. is laughing too hard to answer.)

YOU: . . . and I thought perhaps . . .

C.C. (gasping for breath): Let me guess—cost of living?

J.T. (hysterical): C.*C*.!! I'm gonna bust a *gut*!

YOU: Yes, well, a raise—

(J.T. and C.C. shriek with laughter and double up on the floor.)

C.C. (wiping his eyes): Get out of this office! You'll never work in this town again!

There is also the closely related Visualizing in Hindsight (also known as the "stuck tape recorder"), where you endlessly review what you *should* have said, and continuously evaluate and reevaluate the horrible consequences of your pathetic inadequacies as a human being.

Sample Self-evaluation

I should never have told that joke.
I hope they understood it was a joke.
What if they thought I was serious?
What if one of them was Polish?
I am a failure and everyone hates me.

See how useful this procedure can be?

You could always have done, or at least *said*, something far more satisfactory. Go over and over it in your mind. Remember, inassertiveness followed by self-excoriation is the life's blood of stress!

81

> **STRESS DROPOUT—**
> **MIDWESTERN DIVISION**
> "Once a decision was made,
> I did not worry about it
> afterward."
>
> —HARRY TRUMAN, in his
> *Memoirs*

Elevator Facts 'n' Fallacies

As we get more and more sophisticated in our search for stress, it's sometimes all too easy to overlook the simpler sources—garden-variety stress inducers that are often right under our noses. For example, let's not forget one of the most easily found sources of stress—the common everyday elevator.

Elevators can be operated by anyone, male or female, and can be found almost everywhere. Even the smallest two-story building can provide you with a fully adequate elevator experience.

As in flying, all you really need is a basic understanding of the physics involved. We've provided here a list of some of the most common myths and misconceptions—some of which, as you'll see, turn out to be true!

(1) "An elevator can go through the roof." FACT. Watch out for overly rapid ascension, especially in small buildings.

(2) "Elevator cables can easily snap, sending an elevator plummeting to the basement and crushing you in a splintered mass of steel and glass." FALLACY. You would be crushed in a splintered mass of aluminum and other metal alloys, sometimes even wood. Elevators are rarely made of steel.

(3) "Even one person over the maximum advised occupancy can cause the cables to snap." FACT. What's more, those "maximum number of people" notices are predicated on *thin* people. And they always allow for a few children, too. So if it says eighteen people, probably more like *nine* is the *real* maximum.

(4) "An elevator can be struck by lightning, incinerating the occupants in a massive, raging ball of flame." FALLACY. Where *do* people get these ridiculous ideas, I wonder? The only time you need to worry is if the elevator has gone through the roof (see number 1, above) during an electrical storm. Of course, lightning can, and frequently *does*, strike the elevator *cables* (see number 2, above).

(5) "Elevators are completely enclosed, with no ventilation, and you can easily run out

of air." FACT. We've all seen those signs that say "There is little danger of running out of air. . . ." You'll notice they don't say "there is *no* danger," do they? Ask yourself—why did they bring it up at all? Obviously it is all too easy, in a stalled elevator or even during a long elevator ride, to run out of air and slowly suffocate, choking and clawing at the air like some gaping fish out of water, only an empty shaft as witness to your final strangled cries.

(6) "In a bank of elevators, an elevator can swing sideways, colliding with an adjacent elevator." FACT. This little-known but frequent phenomenon is most prevalent in windy cities.

(7) "Are you saying, forget riding an elevator in the Sears Towers?" ANSWER. This is a Fact 'n' Fallacy format, *not* Question-Answer, stupid.

Noise

YOU ARE probably already aware of one of the most common and accessible sources of stress, Noise. Coupled with Fear of Telling the Neighbors to Shut Up, it constitutes an Ongoing Stress, especially if you *have* asked the neighbors to turn their blaring stereo down and their idea of an appropriate response is "Shut up yourself, ya jerk!" Now, Fear of Bodily Harm may be added to the stress melting pot!

The most easily found Noise Form is, of course, Large Noise:

(1) Blaring TV, radio, or stereo
(2) Screaming children
(3) Screaming adults

These can often be combined with Specialty Large Noise:

(1) Religious chanting* (which involves Great Hesitation to Complain)

(2) Loud and violent punk rock (which involves Even Greater, and Smarter, Hesitation to Complain)

If, for some reason, you're having trouble locating Large Noise, don't overlook its lesser-known relative, Small Noise. Small Noise, if judiciously applied, can be every bit as stress inducing as its larger cousin:

(1) Gum cracking
(2) Knuckle cracking
(3) Tuneless humming
(4) Tooth sucking
(5) Nails on a blackboard
(6) Loud open-mouthed food chewing

and who could forget the ever-popular

(7) Sniffling and throat clearing (phlegm is our friend)

As you can see, the Disgust Quotient (D.Q.) more than makes up for any lack in decibel level.

Small Noise can usually be found with a minimum of effort—in fact, it often seeks *you* out. It is most effective in small, enclosed spaces, so spend as much time as possible in shopping-mall elevators.

*Available only in New York or Los Angeles. Void where prohibited.

A True Story to Contemplate When Thinking About Asking Your Neighbors to Shut Up

G.G. (not even his real *initials*), one of the five big Mafia bosses, was convicted for hitting a man in the head with a baseball bat when the man complained about a noisy party G.G. was attending. G.G. was quoted as saying he wanted to help the man "get some sleep."

Family Occasions

FAMILY occasions are *wonderful* opportunities for stress! Oh, how we love family get-togethers! There's nothing like a good Reverting-to-your-Childhood-Self!

Here are some tips to exploit the full potential of these gatherings:

(1) Bring up every grievance you ever had against your parents. Concentrate on your teen years.

(2) Fight with your siblings. Remind the youngest members of the family how much fun it was before they came along. (If you *are* the youngest, complain to your parents that the others are bullying you.)

(3) Use a lot of sentences beginning with "you always" or "you never."

(4) If there are non-family members present, encourage your parents to recount embarrassing anecdotes about your childhood. (The time you wet your pants in school is always a favorite.)

(5) Meditate on the differences between your childhood ambitions and your actual adult achievements.

(6) Overeat.

How to Inject Stress into Any Fantasy

ANY COMMON worry-wart knows how to fantasize about tax audits, fatal diseases, or being a passenger on the *Hindenburg*. But a true stresser must also know how to introduce stress into even the most utopian fantasies.

For example, let's suppose you see a want ad for the job of your dreams—exciting, high-paying, glamorous. Imagine yourself having the job. Imagine yourself rich, successful, famous. Imagine how your friends will respond to you in your new position of glory.

Will you still be on the same terms with them, though? What about the friends who will *resent* your great success? Imagine yourself spending the money. How easy it is to run up debts! Some of those collection agencies are Mafia-run, you know!

See?

Here are a few specific fantasies to help you on your way.

Female

The man of your dreams strides toward you. With a manly grunt of desire, he roughly takes you in his arms. What are you wearing? The little red dress? Doesn't it make you look fat? And it's sleeveless! Did you remember to shave under your arms? Not to mention deodorant! P.U.!!

Male

The woman of your dreams drifts toward you. With a maidenly sigh of passion, she slowly melts in your arms. What is she wearing? The little red dress? It makes her look fat! And it's sleeveless! Gorilla time! Not to mention—*P.U.*!!

Small Boy

Yankee Stadium. Sold out. You're wearing your Yankee pinstripes. As you come out onto the field, the crowd rises to its feet, shouting, cheering only for you. You stride to the microphone and say: "Today I consider myself-self-self the luckiest man-man-man on the face of the earth-earth-earth. . . ."

Stress on Your
Vacation

A TRUE stresser, of
course, never takes vacations (see "They're Getting Ahead of You"). But sometimes you slip, and
before you know it, you're sunning yourself on the
deck of a luxury cruise ship.

Don't worry! Before you can say *"Andrea
Doria,"* you can easily come up with a whole new
supply of stress opportunities. Soon you may even
prefer vacations for their ever-widening supply of
anxiety!

Your first question, of course, is: *What should
you do?*

The traditional activity for a stress vacation is
worrying about things at home. Did you turn off
the stove? Is the back door locked? What about the
refrigerator—did you close it properly?

Don't forget your job—what about all the

work you should be doing, and all the work you will have to do when you get back? What about your rival? What will he be doing in your absence?

If you have a phone machine, bring along your remote-control beeper so you can pay long-distance charges to be reminded of unpleasant personal problems or, better yet, to confirm that no one ever calls you.

You can also *worry about things on your vacation*—for example, the cost of your hotel room. Can you really afford it? If you weren't such a failure, you could. What about that little glass hot-water pot that comes with the packets of instant coffee? Couldn't you electrocute yourself?

And what about that strange-looking heater? Are you sure it's not emitting asphyxiating gases? Remember that headache you woke up with? Fresh air helped, didn't it? Are you sure you want to go to sleep tonight? Carbon monoxide is odorless, isn't it? What exactly *is* irreversible brain damage? If you had it, would you know? What do they really mean by "check-out time"?

You may also wish to participate in the other stress-vacation activities—complaining, getting sunburned, and trying to figure out how to use those tiny shoeshine cloths in your hotel room.

Or perhaps you'd like to visit the nearby amusement park. Remember that spinning carnival ride, the one where the hydraulic system failed, hurling screaming riders from its cars?

But before you start thinking about what you should do, you must make a much more important decision: *How should you get there?*

Be sure to consider all the options before you decide! Boat trips, of course, offer the possibilities of icebergs, nuclear submarines, and fire at sea, along with the concomitant being trapped on the bottom deck and sinking endless fathoms through the icy coiling depths to your watery grave. Trains offer derailing or collisions. (Flying, of course, is dealt with in a separate chapter.)

But for a true stress vacation, it's hard to beat a good old-fashioned car trip. Not only can you spend your entire trip cramped in a sitting position, worrying about getting hopelessly lost in some out-of-the-way bayou, but you can also enjoy the ongoing stress of driving an unfamiliar car on unknown terrain.

Don't forget:

(1) Wheel can come off at high speed, sending car slamming into cement pylon.
(2) Luggage rack can tilt car's balance, sending car careening off high cliff to be dashed to pieces on the cruel rocks below.
(3) Car can be struck from behind and explode.
(4) Worst stress of all—car can skid, forcing you to try to figure out exactly what "turn wheels into skid" really means.

Even more important, though, in a car trip you also face the prospect of *sharing* your stress with an equally cramped group of strangers, friends, or relatives. Choose your companions carefully. For lengthy trips—say, across the southern United States in midsummer, without air conditioning—the true stresser's choice is always *traveling with your parents and siblings.* (See also "Family Occasions.") If you're female, this is a good time to tell them of your decision to move in with your boyfriend. If you're male, even better.

And don't forget to include the family cat. Nothing punctuates endless raving family arguments better than the low maniacal caterwauling of an overheated feline.

Sample Vacation Conversation

FATHER: You'll never forgive yourself!
MOTHER: You're throwing your life away!
YOU: I am *not*!
BROTHER: Why don't you all just shut up!
YOU: *You* shut up!
BROTHER: No, *you* shut up!
SISTER: I have to go to the *bath*room—
CAT: UlulululululAAAAAAOOOOWWWWWW . . .

But as important as it is to decide what to do and how to get there, there is another decision of even greater consequence. We're talking, of course, about your destination: *Where should you go?*

This is perhaps your most far-reaching decision, the one that will most affect the quality of your trip. It depends entirely on your own personal tastes. What are your particular fears, your own pet anxieties?

In California, for example, you can worry about earthquakes, which rumble up from the bowels of the earth and swallow you and your car into gaping chasms. Hawaii has volcanoes spewing out tons of seething fiery lava. Miami has hurricanes. A winter trip to Maine might offer an icy blizzard and the possibility of freezing to death.

But the American heartland offers perhaps the favorite natural disaster of the stresser—tornadoes. Tornadoes not only rear up suddenly from the dusty plains, cutting a giant swath of disaster as though with some monstrous scythe, they also include the ever-popular possibility of *cowering in a basement*. Many of you will recognize this, of course, as the stresser's stance to life.

But what about blizzards, you may ask? They cut swaths too!

Sure, they cut *icy* swaths. But there's no vortex, no horrifying uprush, no sudden darkening of the sky as though the very devil had appeared!

Well, what about hurricanes?

Hurricanes! Chicken feed! You can see them coming for days, people have incredible amounts of time to prepare—you can even get evacuated! Sorry, tornadoes it is.

For the widest palette of stress opportunities, though, many stressers choose to go abroad.

First of all, you have to carry a passport, and it's always nice to have a picture of yourself looking like a cow.

In addition, you can also worry about losing your passport and being stranded on the wrong side of the Berlin Wall, coming down with an obscure parasitic disease and being incarcerated in some sweltering primitive hospital, or being caught in a sudden, bloody civil war—all with the added lure of not understanding a word that anyone says to you!

> **STRESS GRAND MASTER—STEPPES OF ASIA DIVISION**
> **"Departure beyond the borders of my own country is for me equivalent to death."**
>
> —BORIS PASTERNAK, in a letter

As you can see, traveling offers a cornucopia of new stress stimuli—perhaps even more than at home. Soon you may find yourself actually looking forward to your vacations as uniquely harrowing times of dread. *Bon voyage!*

Procrastination as a Source of Stress

WE STILL don't have time to discuss this right now.

Conclusion

A s you can see, stress and stress by-products can easily be yours. For example, right as you are reading this, you should be feeling:

(1) Anxiety at the time you spent reading this book when you should have been working

(2) Anxiety that the book is ending and now you have to go back to work and probably fail

(3a) Money worries after buying this book

or

(3b) Moral worries after shoplifting this book

or

(3c) Legal worries after having been *caught* shoplifting this book

(4) A strange nagging headache, probably the forerunner of a cerebral hemorrhage.

Good! Now that you've recognized your stress potential, with a little effort, you can adroitly maneuver your ship of life through ever-expanding horizons of stress.

What about backsliding, you might ask? What about those particularly bad moments, those curves life sometimes throws you?

First of all, the very fact that you are *worrying in advance* is an excellent sign of stress mastery.

Second, always remember: In an emergency, *apply one of the Basic Stress Concepts.*

Suppose you're watching *Top Hat,* or listening to *Don Giovanni,* or bathing in the glow of an iridescent Caribbean sunset, and you find yourself relentlessly, inexorably relaxing?

Just remember—Fred got ahead of you! I don't see *you* practicing until your toes bleed. *Mozart* got ahead of you by the time he was four! And as for the sunset, *well*—created any worlds lately?

See how simple it is?

If you nevertheless, despite all your efforts, find yourself relaxing, you can always join R.A.— Relaxers Anonymous, a new self-help organization. They will assign you a "stress buddy" whom you can call in moments of unexpected well-being. He will talk you down, reminding you of the many ways you have failed in the past and the many opportunities for misery and squalid depression in the future. "You *are* worthless. I don't care if you did win the Nobel Prize. You can never again achieve those heights."

Just remember the R.A. slogan: "Take it many, many days at a time." No matter how well things are going, there's always something bad you can worry about.

**STRESS GRAND MASTER—
TEUTONIC DIVISION**
"Hence, in whatever case
you may be, it is well to
picture to yourself the
opposite: in prosperity, to
be mindful of misfortune; in
friendship, of enmity; in
good weather, of days when
the sky is overcast; in love,
of hatred; in moments of
trust, to imagine the
betrayal that will make you
regret your confidence . . ."

—ARTHUR SCHOPENHAUER, in
Counsels and Maxims

Remember, you *are* a failure. Everyone *does* hate you.

Stress is work, and you must be working at it twenty-four hours a day. Your proper goal is not just to be stressed, but to be *more* stressed than anyone else. As in everything else you do, you must be perfect! Every effort you make must succeed! And always remember the stress motto:

If at first you don't succeed, you have failed.